overcoming
speechlessness

overcoming speechlessness

A POET ENCOUNTERS THE HORROR
IN RWANDA, EASTERN CONGO, AND
PALESTINE/ISRAEL

alice walker

Seven Stories Press
NEW YORK

A Seven Stories Press First Edition

Seven Stories Press
140 Watts Street
New York, NY 10013
www.sevenstories.com

In Canada: Publishers Group Canada, 559 College Street, Suite 402, Toronto, ON M6G 1A9

In the UK: Turnaround Publisher Services Ltd., Unit 3, Olympia Trading Estate, Coburg Road, Wood Green, London N22 6TZ

In Australia: Palgrave Macmillan, 15–19 Claremont Street, South Yarra, VIC 3141

College professors may order examination copies of Seven Stories Press titles for a free six-month trial period. To order, visit www.sevenstories.com/textbook or send a fax on school letterhead to (212) 226-1411.

Book design by Jon Gilbert

Library of Congress Cataloging-in-Publication Data

Walker, Alice, 1944-
  Overcoming speechlessness : a poet encounters the horror in Rwanda, Eastern Congo, and Palestine/Israel / Alice Walker. -- 1st ed.
     p. cm.
  ISBN 978-1-58322-917-0 (pbk.)
  1. Walker, Alice, 1944---Travel--Rwanda. 2. Walker, Alice, 1944---Travel--Congo (Democratic Republic) 3. Walker, Alice, 1944---Travel--Gaza Strip. 4. Rwanda--Social conditions. 5. Congo (Democratic Republic)--Social conditions. 6. Gaza Strip--Social conditions. 7. West Bank--Social conditions. 8. Atrocities. I. Title.
  PS3573.A425Z469 2010
  306.6--dc22   2009047607

Printed in the USA

9 8 7 6 5 4 3 2 1

Three things cannot be hidden: the sun, the moon, and the truth.
—*Buddha*

1. THREE YEARS AGO

Three years ago I visited Rwanda and eastern Congo. In Kigali I paid my respects to the hundreds of thousands of infants, toddlers, teenagers, adolescents, young engaged couples, married people, women and men, grandmothers and grandfathers, brothers and sisters of every facial shape and body size, who had been hacked into sometimes quite small pieces by armed strangers, or by neighbors, or by acquaintances and "friends" they knew. These bodies and pieces of bodies are now neatly and respectfully buried in mass graves. Fifteen years ago these graves were encircled by cuttings of plants that are now sturdy, blossoming vines that cover their iron trellises with flowers. Inside the adjacent museum there are photographs of the murdered: their open smiles or wise and consoling eyes will remain with me always. There is also, in the museum, a brief history of Rwanda. It tells of the long centuries Tutsi and Hutu lived together, intermarrying and raising their children, until the coming of the Belgians in the 1800s. (Before the Belgians, the territory had been colonized by the Germans.) The Belgian settlers determined with the measurements of Hutu and Tutsi skulls that the Tutsi were more intelligent than the Hutu, more like Europeans, and therefore placed the Tutsi above the Hutu. Over a hundred years later, when the Belgian colonists left for Europe, and after many changes to each of these groups, they left the Hutu in charge. The hatred this diabolical decision caused between these formerly coexisting peoples festered over generations, coming to a lethal boil in the tragedy of genocide.

I had done research while in college and written a thesis of sorts on the "Belgian" Congo, where King Leopold of Belgium introduced the policy of cutting off the hands of enslaved Africans who didn't or couldn't fulfill their rubber quota. They were collecting latex for the rubber that made tires for the new cars everyone was beginning to want in America and Europe; I had not known that these same activities had spread into the Kingdom of Rwanda. To the Belgians, apparently, and to the German colonialists before them, it was all one vast "empty" territory to be exploited without any consideration for the people living there. Indigenous Africans didn't seem to exist, except as slaves.

While visiting the set for the film *The Color Purple*, many decades after college, a sad older man from Africa, who had been a doctor in the Congo and was now hired as an extra for our film, lamented the loss of his country, his people, and his land, telling me that the Firestone Corporation had taken millions of acres of land, "leasing" it for pennies an acre, in perpetuity. The people who'd lived there since the beginning of humanity had been forced to tend the trees planted

there on Firestone's vast rubber tree planta-
tion. I immediately thought of every car I'd
owned and all the tires that ran under them.

2. FROM KIGALI

From Kigali and meetings with survivors,
witnessing their courage and fortitude, their
willingness to move on and beyond
unspeakable tragedy, I went to eastern
Congo. There I met with women still vic-
timized by the killers of Kigali, who had
been chased across the border into their
country. These women had been the victims
of rape on so large a scale—rape as one of
the cruelest weapons of war—it seemed
impossible they had not, in their despair,
chosen to destroy themselves. Their villages
had frequently turned against them because
of the abuse they had experienced; if their
husbands were still alive, they regularly dis-
missed them, refusing them shelter in their
own homes.

One beautiful woman, who came to meet me wearing white and purple, had been a sex slave in the bush for over a year, forced to carry loads that bent her double, her eyes repeatedly struck to damage her vision so that she would not be able to identify her assailants, her whole body beaten until, over a year later, there was still a discernible limp when she attempted to walk with what one assumed was her former grace. We embraced each other with tears, and with joy. I was more thankful to see her radiant resurrection than I had been to witness anything in my life. She had been raped with every imaginable instrument, including machete handles and gun barrels. Thanks to you, my sisters of Women for Women International, she said, I have come through. Many of us have come through. We will not go back. We will not be slaves and beasts of burden.

Over 4 million Congolese have been murdered in an endless war whose foundation rests on the mineral wealth of the

Congo. One of those minerals, coltan, makes cell phone use possible. Millions of families are homeless and in ruin, living in the rain and heat. War continues, like a sickness that has no cure. Infectious diseases are rampant. Weapons flow into the hands of the young, even into the hands of children. How can she smile? I wonder about my just-met Congolese sister. She does so because she is alive, which means the Feminine is alive.

There is the work of the Mother to do.

There is the work of the Daughter to do.

This is a source of joy. We embrace, parting. She will learn how to start a business and longs to take lessons in computer use.

3. COMING HOME

Coming home I found that I could talk about this woman, and, indeed, she would later come to America and talk about herself. She understood the importance of speech, speech about the unspeakable, and is a source of my ability to share the following story, a story that had propelled me into a period of speechlessness. While in Congo we were invited to visit a young woman, my own daughter's age at the time, thirty-six, who was in a local hospital. When we first saw Generose, she was lying on a pallet on the floor in an outer passageway, waiting for us. Taking up her crutch, she led us to a quiet area at the back of the hospital where we sat circled around her as she told her story. Her story was this: Her village had been terrorized by the Interharmwe murderers (presumably Hutu) who had been chased out of Rwanda by the Tutsi forces of Paul Kagame (now president of Rwanda); the suffering had been unbearable as people were chased from their homes at all hours of the day or night, many of them choosing to sleep in the forest or to hide in their own fields.

Generose was home with her husband and two children because her husband was sick. One evening there was a fierce knock at the door, and gunmen who also carried machetes entered demanding food. There was little to offer them but the staple diet: a boiled vegetable (that to my eyes, being shown it in the fields earlier, looked like okra leaves) and a few balls of steamed millet. The men ate this but were angry and not satisfied. They went and found her husband, still in bed, and hacked him to pieces on the spot. They came back to Generose and her children and took hold of her. Holding her down, they began to cut off her leg. They cut off her leg, cut it into six pieces, and began to fry it in a pan. When some part of it seemed nearly done, they tried to force her son to take a bite. Strongly, beautifully, and so much the son of our dreams, he said: No, I will never eat my mother's flesh. They shot him to death without more conversation. The daughter, seeing this, watching her mother bleeding to death, knowing her father had been hacked to pieces, was now offered the same opportunity. Terrorized, she bit into a piece of her mother's body. Her mother, having crawled away, does not know what became of her. Though she does know that her assailants went next door that same evening and murdered a couple who'd been married that day, raping and mutilating the bride, tearing out her eyes.

This was the child Generose was hoping we could help her find. Apparently she had escaped after this gruesome torture, and now, where could she be? Generose hoped for only two things from us: that we help her find her daughter (beyond our capacity, probably, though Women for Women International would try) and that we help her start a small business, so that when her daughter is found she can provide a safe place for them to live. A proud woman who reminded me of a young Toni Morrison, she did not once stammer in the telling of her tale, though those of us around her felt a quaking in the heart. I have not for a moment forgotten this child who was forced to bite into her mother's flesh. Yet it has been almost impossible to speak of it.

Coming home I fell ill with the burden of this story, as I had fallen ill after reading in the *New York Times* a year or so earlier of similar torture used against the so-called "pygmies" of Africa's rainforests ("pygmies" because in ancient Egyptian the word means *elbow high*). In order to frighten them away from their homes, to ultimately make way for lumbering and mining interests located in the West, mercenaries were indoctrinating their soldiers to believe that killing pygmies and eating their hearts would make the soldiers invisible and capable, as the smaller people seemed to be, of evading capture by blending with their environment. Reading this story I felt as if my own heart had been taken out of me, and this assault on the planetary human body that I represent brought me low.

4. SANGHA

I was fortunate to have a *sangha*, a Buddhist circle of support, to which I could eventually turn. Sitting around me as I talked, two of our members realized I needed even more of a healing than simply being able to speak about what I had witnessed and heard of what is happening to the people of the earth. They immediately devised a ritual for my care. Placing me on the green grass of my yard, surrounding me with flowers, stones, photographs of those who comfort us (I placed several under my blouse: John Lennon, Pema Chödrön, Howard Zinn, the Dalai Lama, Amma, and Che among them), and their own loving words, they helped me shed tears of hopelessness, as I asked myself and them: What has happened to humanity? More tears of resolve followed. Because whatever has happened to humanity, whatever is currently happening to humanity, it is happening to all of us.

No matter how hidden the cruelty, no

matter how far off the screams of pain and terror, we live in one world. We are one people. My illness proved that. As well as my understanding that Generose's lost daughter belongs to all of us. It is up to all of us to find her; it is up to us to do our best to make her whole again.

There is only one daughter, one father, one mother, one son, one aunt or uncle, one dog, one cat, donkey, monkey, or goat in the universe, after all: the one right in front of you.

5. ONCE AGAIN

And so I have been, once again, struggling to speak about an atrocity: this time in Gaza, this time against the Palestinian people. Like most people on the planet, I have been aware of the Palestinian–Israeli conflict almost my whole life.

I was four years old in 1948 when, after being subjected to unspeakable cruelty by the Germans, after a holocaust so many future disasters would resemble, thousands of European Jews were resettled in Palestine. They settled in a land that belonged to people already living there, which did not seem to bother the British who, as with India, had occupied Palestine and then, on leaving it, helped put in place a partitioning of the land they thought would work fine for the people, strangers, Palestinians and European Jews, now forced to live together.

When we witness the misery and brutality that is still a daily reality for millions of people in Pakistan and India, we are looking at the failure, and heartlessness, of the "partition" plan. Though it might be true that the partitioning of what became India and Pakistan came after the insistence of a Muslim leader, Muhammad Ali Jinnah, it is extremely doubtful that separating their millions of people into different countries would have occurred to the Indians, Hindu and Muslim, had England not spent centuries telling each group its misery was the other's fault.

6. WHO WOULD TELL HER?

I got to Gaza the way I have gotten to so many places in my life: a sister called me. My friend, the writer Susan Griffin, with whom I was arrested protesting the start of the war against Iraq in 2003, sent an email. Would I be interested in going to Gaza? With CODEPINK, the women's peace group that had gotten us into such soul-strengthening trouble six years before. She would go, she said, if she could sell the book she was currently writing. This is how so many of us live; I remember this when I look about the world and want more witnesses to the scenes of horror, brutality, chaos. We all have to work to feed ourselves, look after our families, keep our heads above water. I understand this completely—and wasn't sure I was free enough myself to go.

However, it happened that, in the same week that the Israeli military began its twenty-two-day bombardment of Gaza—a refugee camp that became a city and is today a mere sliver of Palestine left to the Palestinians, a city and environs that Israel had laid siege to months before, keeping out food and medicine and building materials, among other necessities—my own sister died after a long illness. Our relationship had been a good one for most of our lives, and then, toward the end of her life, it had become strained. So much so that when she died I had not expected to feel devastation.

Surprise. As I was grieving her loss, I learned of the dropping of bombs on the people of Palestine. Houses, hospitals, factories, police stations, parliament buildings, ministries, apartment buildings, schools went up in dust. The sight of one family, in which five young daughters had been killed, was seared into my consciousness. The mother, wounded and unconscious, was alive. Who would tell her? I waited to hear some word of regret, of grief, of compassion from our leaders in Washington, who had sent the money, the earnings of American taxpayers, to buy the bombs destroying her world. The little concern voiced from our "leaders" was faint, arrived late, was delivered without much feeling, and was soon overshadowed by an indifference to the value of Palestinian life that has corrupted our children's sense of right and wrong for generations. Later our government would offer money, a promise to help "rebuild." As if money and rebuilding were the issues. If someone killed my children and offered me money for the privilege of having done so, I would view them as monsters, not humanitarians.

I consulted my companion, who did not hesitate. We must go, he said. The sooner we reach the people of Gaza, the sooner they'll know not all Americans are uncaring, deaf and blind, or fooled by the media. He quoted Abraham Lincoln: You can fool some of the people all of the time, and all of the people some of the time, but you can not fool all of the people all of the time.

Americans have been deliberately misled by our government and by the media about the reality and *meaning* of events in the Middle East; this is especially true where Palestine and Israel are concerned. Our ignorance has cost us dearly. The feeling of having been taken, *fooled*, and of still being taken, for a very expensive ride is quite galling, especially as we see our own society collapsing from lack of the same attention we give to Israel: subsidized housing, for instance, and protection of our neighborhoods. There is actual puzzlement in most people's minds about why "the state of Israel" consumes far more interest, funding, and news coverage than, say, my own former state, Georgia, or the state where I live now, California. Americans are generally uninformed about the reality of this never-ending "conflict" that has puzzled us for decades and of which so many of us, if we are honest, are heartily sick.

We began to pack.

7. A LONG WAY TO GAZA

It's a long way to Gaza. Flying between San Francisco and Frankfurt, then from Frankfurt into Egypt, I kept my mind focused by meditating as much as possible, reading Aung San Suu Kyi and Alan Clements's book, *The Voice of Hope*, thinking about Desmond Tutu and his courageous statement earlier in the month about the immorality of the walls Israel has built around Palestinian villages as well as the immorality of the siege itself. I had read President Jimmy Carter's book, *Palestine: Peace Not Apartheid*, before leaving home. I also ate a good bit of chocolate. And slept.

Arriving in Cairo at 3:30 a.m., my first task, assigned to me prior to the trip by the beautiful, indomitable, and well-loved cofounder of CODEPINK, Medea Benjamin, was to meet with her and the US ambassador to Egypt, Ambassador Margaret Scobey, at 10:30 a.m. to ask for assistance in crossing the border into Gaza from Egypt. After a few hours' rest, I appeared early for the meeting (concerned that Medea had not arrived yet) which, though cordial, would yield no help. Even so, I was able to have an interesting talk with the ambassador about the use of nonviolence. She—a white woman with a Southern accent—mentioned the success of "our" civil rights movement and asked why couldn't the Palestinians be more like us. It was a remarkable comment from a perspective of unimaginable safety and privilege; I was moved to tell her of the effort it took, even for someone so inherently nonviolent as me, to contain myself during seven years in Mississippi when it often appeared there were only a handful of white Mississippians who could talk to a person of color without delivering injury or insult. If we had not been able to change our situation through nonviolent suffering, we would have most certainly, like the African National Congress (ANC), like the Palestine Liberation Organization (PLO), like Hamas, turned to violence. I told her how dishonest it seemed to me that people claim not to understand the desperate, last-ditch resistance involved in suicide bombings, blaming the oppressed for using their bodies where the Israeli army uses armored tanks.

I remembered aloud, we being Southerners, my own anger at the humiliations, bomb-ings, assassinations that made weeping an endless activity for black people for cen-turies, and how when we would finally get to a courtroom that was supposed to offer justice, the judge would likely blame us for the crime done against us and call us chim-panzees for making a fuss. Medea arrived at this point, having been kept circling the building in a taxi that never landed, and pressed our case for entry into Gaza. While appearing sympathetic to our petition, our ambassador emphasized it was dangerous for us to go into Gaza and that her office would be powerless to help us if we arrived there and were injured or stranded. We were handed some papers telling us all the reasons we should not go.

8. PASTRAMI FROM "THE BUTCHER"

Next we were at a strange ministry whose name never registered, to fill out forms whose intent escaped me. Several CODE-PINK women were already there, waiting their turn for the bit of paper we needed to move a step closer to the Egyptian border crossing at Rafah, maybe the only one available to us. There I met a CODEPINKer who instantly made me happy to be with CODE-PINK again. She'd been waiting for hours, felt she was growing into her chair, and we laughed at the absurdity of bureaucracy everywhere, which keeps you waiting interminably for some bit of paper that you feel sure will be thrown into the trash or into a creaking file drawer as soon as you leave the room, never again to see the light of day.

I reconnected with Gael Murphy, who reminded me we had shared a paddy wagon after being arrested in front of the White House a few days before George W. Bush started his ill-fated war on the people and animals, rivers and dwellings, mosques and libraries of Iraq. She handed me an illustrated postcard that showed plainly what the situation between Israel and Palestine had come down to: in 1946 the Palestinians owned Palestine, by their numbers, though Britain ruled it, with a few scattered Jewish villages (picture one); some years later under a United Nations plan for partitioning, Palestine and Israel each owned roughly half of the land (picture two); from 1949 to 1967 the Israel "half" grew by about a third; after the Six-Day War of 1967, Israel doubled its land mass by virtue of the land it took from Palestine at that time. The last picture showed the situation in 2008: Palestinian refugees (in their own country) living in camps in the West Bank and Gaza, with the whole land now called Israel. On the back of this card were words from former Israeli president Ariel Sharon, known as the "Butcher of Sabra and Shatila" (refugee camps in Lebanon where he led a massacre of the people), where he talked about making a pastrami sandwich of the Palestinian people, riddling their lands with Jewish settlements until no one would be able to imagine a whole Palestine. Or would know Palestine ever existed.

9. TURTLE ISLAND

No one can imagine a whole Turtle Island, either, now known as the United States of America, but formerly the land of indigenous peoples. The land of some of my native ancestors, the Cherokee, whose homes and villages were obliterated from the landscape where they'd existed for millennia; the Cherokee who were forced—those who remained—to resettle, walking the Trail of Tears, a thousand miles away.

This is familiar territory, as is the treatment of the Palestinian people. On the bus ride through the Egyptian desert toward the Rafah gate, which leads into Palestine, I think about this particular cycle of violence humans have made for themselves.

Hitler learned (partly) from the Americans how to "cleanse" Germany of the Jews, even how to use Jewish hair to stuff mattresses. Indian hair had been mattress stuffing long before. Indian skin made into various objects. Indian children and families, massacred. Not because they were "savages"—one glance at their art told anyone who they were—but because the European settlers who came to America wanted their land. Just as the Israelis have wanted, and have taken by force, Palestinian land. Like Americans they have attempted to hide their avarice and cruelty behind a mountain of myths: that no one lived in Palestine, that the Palestinians are savages, that there's no such thing as a Palestinian (Golda Meir's offering), that the

Israelis are David and the Palestinians Goliath. Which is ridiculous, if you haven't been indoctrinated against the Palestinians for centuries from reading the Bible where, as the Philistines (we are taught) they are forever causing trouble for God's children, the Hebrews. Then there's Hollywood, which has a lot to answer for in its routine disregard for Arabs generally, but which, where Palestine and Israel are concerned, projects Israel as always in the right, no matter what it does, as American politicians, for the most part, have learned to do. This is not good for Israel or for the United States, just as always praising the regrettable behavior of one's child, or of anyone, can only lead to disaster. A disaster, where Israel is concerned, that is happening before our eyes, even if the media in America refuses to let Americans fully see it.

I had not been on a bus with so many Jews since traveling by Greyhound to the 1963 March on Washington, where Martin Luther King Jr., John Lewis, and others spoke so passionately of black Americans' determination to be free. On this bus I went with a young half-Jewish man named, not so ironically when I later thought of it, David. He was not considered really Jewish because his mother was Irish Catholic, and you could only be a real Jew if your mother were Jewish. I didn't know that then. I had thought his behavior, coming to the side of the oppressed, very Jewish. It was fairly Irish, too, but at the time the Irish in Boston, except for the Kennedys, seemed far from their tradition in this area. They were regularly stoning and/or shouting obscenities at black children who tried to attend "their" schools.

It was moving to hear the stories of why the Jews on our Gaza-bound bus were going to Palestine. Many of them simply said they couldn't bear the injustice, or the hypocrisy. Having spoken out against racism, terrorism, apartheid elsewhere, how could they be silent about Palestine and Israel? Someone said her friends claimed everyone who spoke out against Israeli treatment of Palestinians was a self-hating Jew (if Jewish) or anti-Semitic (though Palestinians are Semites, too). She said it never seemed to dawn on the persons making the anti-Semitic charge that it is Israel's behavior people are objecting to and not its religion. As for being self-hating? Well, she said, I actually love myself too much as a Jew to pretend to be ignorant about something so obvious. Ignorance is not held in high regard in Jewish culture.

One story that particularly moved me was this: A woman in her late fifties or early sixties stood at the front of the bus, as we passed donkey carts and Mercedes Benzes, and spoke of traveling to Palestine without her husband, a Jewish man who was born in Palestine. Several times they had come back to Palestine, renamed Israel, to see family.

To attend graduations, weddings, and funerals. Each time they were held for hours at the airport as her husband was stripped, searched, interrogated, and threatened when he spoke up for himself. In short, because his passport was stamped with the place of his birth, Palestine, he was treated like a Palestinian. This Jewish husband sent his best wishes, but he could no longer endure travel in so painful a part of the world.

By now most of us are aware of the dehumanizing treatment anyone not Jewish receives on crossing a border into Israel, especially brutal for Palestinians. I thought: Even our new president, Barack Hussein Obama, were he just anybody and not the president of the United States, would have a humiliating time getting into Israel. The poet and rebel in me instantly wanted him to try it. To don the clothing of an average person, as truth-seeking people do in wisdom tales, and travel into Israel. To learn what is real and true, not by traveling through the air, but by walking on the ground.

11. RIDING ON THE BUS

Riding on the bus, listening to the stories of people drawn to the side of the Palestinian people, I leaned into the landscape. Mile after mile of barren desert went by, with scatterings of villages and towns. The farther into the Sinai we went the more poverty we saw. One sight in particular has stayed with me: the Bedouin, formerly the nomads of the desert, attempting to live alongside the road or on the barren hills, sometimes in dwellings made of sticks and straw, without their camels, without mobility.

Occasionally lone women in flowing black robes walked along a ridge in the heat, going someplace not visible to the eye. Hundreds of tiny white brick buildings, most unfinished, studded the hills. I asked my friend: What do you think those small white buildings are? He said: Bunkers. Mausoleums? But no, seeing them appear in all manner and stage of construction, over hundreds of miles, I saw that they were poor peoples' attempts at building housing for themselves. They looked like bunkers and mausoleums because no one was around them, and because they were so small: some of them barely large enough to lie down in, and often with no windows, only a door. I realized that people who worked far away and were able to return only sporadically were building them. This is true of many places in the world, and I was moved by the tenacity of people trying to have a home, no matter how uprooted or displaced they have been. Creating and having a home is a primary instinct in humankind, in all of nature; seeing these tiny dwellings, with no water sources, no electricity, no anything but white mud bricks, made me remember my own childhood feelings of insecurity around housing and the preciousness of having a home, as we were forced to move year after year.

12. RACHEL'S PARENTS, CINDY AND CRAIG

I came out of this reverie to hear the story of Cindy and Craig Corrie, the parents of Rachel Corrie, who were traveling with us. Rachel Corrie was murdered when she tried to stop an Israeli tank from demolishing a Palestinian house. I was struck by her parents' beauty and dignity. Cindy's face radiated resolve and kindness, Craig's a study in acceptance, humility, incredible strength, and perseverance. Rachel had been working in Palestine and witnessed the ruthlessness of the deliberate destruction of Palestinian homes by the Israeli army, most surrounded by gardens or small orchards of orange and olive trees, which the army consistently uprooted. No doubt believing that the sight of a young Jewish woman in a brightly colored jumpsuit would stop the soldier in the tank, she placed herself between the home of her Palestinian friends and the tank. It rolled over her, crushing her body and breaking her back. The Corries spoke of their continued friendship with the family who had lived in that house.

Everywhere we went, after arriving in Gaza, locals greeted the Corries with compassion and tenderness. This was particularly moving to me because of the connection I was able to make with another such sacrifice decades ago in Mississippi, in 1967, and how black people became aware that there were some white people who actually cared about what was happening to them. The "three civil rights workers," as they became known, were James Chaney, a young African-American Christian man, and Andrew Goodman and Michael Schwerner, both white Jewish men from the North.

The Northerners had been called to the civil rights movement in the South by their conscience, having watched the racist and sadistic treatment of black people there. The three young men were riding through the backwoods of Neshoba County, Mississippi, when their car was firebombed. They were dragged from the car, bludgeoned and shot to death; their bodies were buried in a dam that was under construction in the area and would not be found for months. While America waited for the bodies to be found, black and white people working for black liberation in the South discovered new ground. Who could not love these young men, all three of them, for risking their lives to change ours? And so, in every church, every Sunday, prayers went out for James, yes, but also for Michael and Andrew. They became ours, just as the Corries have become family to the Palestinian people.

This is one of the most beautiful passages for human beings. It is as if we enter a different door of our reality, when someone gives her or his life for us. Why this should be is a mystery, but it is the mystery, I think, behind all the great myths in which there is human sacrifice—not on an altar but on the road, in the street—for the common good.

At a meeting of the Veterans of the Mississippi Civil Rights Movement held in Jackson, Mississippi, last year, I saw the widow of Michael Schwerner. There she was, over forty years later. There she was, still belonging to her own people, and still, also, one of us.

13. MOTHER FORCE

We arrived in the Gaza Strip in the afternoon, after being kept at the border crossing for about five hours. Long enough to become accustomed to the bombing, someone informed us, is a constant just inside the Palestinian border, reminding the Palestinians of the Israeli presence during the cease-fire. I had never been so close to bombs being dropped before, and I took the opportunity to interrogate my life. Had I lived it the best way I could?

A young Palestinian man, Abdullah X, a student of video at a school in Egypt, had joined us. He had managed to leave Palestine on scholarship to go to school in Cairo three years earlier. Because of the siege and all borders being closed, he had not been able to see his family. He had not seen them for three years. Because of Israel's bombardment of Gaza, he feared for the lives of his family and was determined to see them.

Abdullah might have stepped out of ancient Assyria. With large dark eyes, olive complexion, and hair in curly dark ringlets, he was a striking young man. Between Cairo and the Gaza border, he had, without doing anything special, made many of us on the bus care about him. Sure enough, the Egyptian border patrol gave Abdullah a hard time. When I was told of this by a woman who had stood next to him until ordered away by a patrolman, we decided to stand some distance from him, while he seemed to be pleading to be allowed to visit his parents, and to send the mother force, the universal parent force, to speed his liberation. We stood together, closed our eyes, and sent every ounce of our combined energy to Abdullah's back. When he was given his passport and allowed to join us, we cheered. We could only imagine what going back into Gaza meant for him. This was his home, and much of it had been obliterated. We could not know at the time that, coming out of Gaza, Abdullah would be kept at the border crossing, as he had feared, not permitted back into Egypt. We would wait for him, but ultimately we would leave him there. He had realized his education and his future were at risk. But his love of his family, his home, and his land was very strong.

Later we would also have a glimpse of his father and of his relationship with his father. We were moved by the love and affection expressed between them. For what could it mean to know from day to day that you could easily lose each other to the madness of war? A war brought to your door by people who claimed that everything you had, no matter how little was left, was theirs?

14. ROLLING INTO GAZA

Rolling into Gaza City I had a feeling of homecoming. There is a flavor to the ghetto. To the Bantustan. To the "rez." To the "colored section." In some ways it is surprisingly comforting. *Because consciousness is comforting.* Everyone you see has an awareness of struggle, of resistance, just as you do. The man driving the donkey cart. The woman selling vegetables. The young person arranging rugs on the sidewalk or flowers in a vase.

When I lived in segregated Eatonton, Georgia, I used to breathe normally only in my own neighborhood, only in the black section of town. Everywhere else was too dangerous. A friend was beaten and thrown in prison for helping a white girl, in broad daylight, fix her bicycle chain.

But even this sliver of a neighborhood, so rightly named the Gaza Strip, was not safe. It had been bombed for twenty-two days. I thought of how in the US the first and perhaps only bombing of US soil from the air prior to 9/11 was the bombing of a black community in Tulsa, Oklahoma, in the 1920s. The black people who created it were considered, by white racists, too prosperous and therefore "uppity." Everything they created was destroyed. This was followed by the charge already rampant in white American culture, that black people never tried to "better" themselves. There is ample evidence in Gaza that the Palestinians never stop trying to "better" themselves. What started as a refugee camp with tents has evolved into a city with buildings rivaling those in almost any other city in the "developing" world. There are houses, apartment buildings, schools, mosques, churches, libraries, hospitals. Driving along the streets we could see right away that many of these were in ruins. I realized I had never understood the true meaning of "rubble." Such and such was "reduced to rubble" is a phrase we hear. It is different seeing what demolished buildings actually look like.

Buildings in which people were living. Buildings from which hundreds of broken bodies have been removed. So thorough a job have the Palestinians done in removing the dead from squashed dwellings that no scent of death remains.

What this task must have been like, both physically and psychologically, staggers the mind. We pass police stations that were simply flattened, and all the young (most Palestinians are young) officers in them killed, hundreds of them. We pass ministries, bombed into fragments. We pass a hospital, bombed and gutted by fire.

If one is not safe in a hospital, when one is already sick and afraid, where is one safe? If children are not safe playing in their schoolyards, where are they safe?

Where are
The World Parents of All Children?
The World Caretakers of All the Sick?

15. TWO SISTERS

My companion and I were assigned to the home of two sisters who shared their space with friends and relatives who came and went. One morning I got up early to find an aunt sleeping on the floor in the living room. Another time, a cousin. In the middle of the night I heard one of the sisters consoling her aged father, who sounded disoriented, and helping him back to bed. There was such respect, such tenderness in her voice. This was the same place that, just weeks earlier, was surrounded by rocket fire, a missile landing every twenty-seven seconds for twenty-two days. I could only imagine what the elderly residents must have felt as, even in their old age, they were subjected to so much fear. Each morning we were sent off to learn what we could in our four days in Gaza, well fed on falafel, hummus, olives, and dates, sometimes eggs, tomatoes, salad, and cheese. All of it simple, all of it delicious.

More delicious because we realized how difficult it was to find such food here; the blockade keeps out most of it. Delicious also because it was shared with such generosity and graciousness. Always the culinary student, I tried to learn to make the especially tasty dish that consists mainly of tomatoes and eggs. I learned the tea I like so much is made out of sage! On International Women's Day, we left for the celebration for which we came, a gathering with the women of Gaza.

16. HATRED AND HEAD SCARVES

Gael Murphy, Medea Benjamin, Susan Griffin, and I, along with twenty or so other women, had been arrested for protesting the war on Iraq on International Women's Day 2003. If the world had paid attention we could have saved a lot of money and countless sons' and daughters' lives, as well as prevented a lot of war-generated pollution that hastens globe-threatening climate change. How doofus humans are going to look—we thought as we marched, sang, accepted our handcuffs—still firing rockets into apartment buildings full of families, and dropping bombs on school children and their pets, when the ice melts completely in the Arctic and puts an end to our regressive, greed-sourced rage forever? That had been a wonderful day; this International Women's Day of 2009 was also. It was the kind of day that makes life, already accepted as a gift, a prize. Early that morning of March 8, we were shuttled to a women's center in the north of Gaza City to meet women who, like their compatriots, had survived the recent bombardment and, so far, the siege.

This center for women was opened under the auspices of the United Nations, which has been administering to the Palestinian people since 1948, when thousands of Palestinians fleeing their homes under

Israeli attack became refugees. It is a modest building with a small library whose shelves hold few books. It isn't clear whether most of the women read. The idea, as it is explained to us, is to offer the women a place to gather outside the home since, in Palestinian culture, the mobility of most women is limited by their work in the home as mothers and caretakers of their families. Many women rarely leave their compounds. But today, International Women's Day, is different. Many women are out and about, and women who frequent this particular center are on hand to welcome us. After arranging ourselves around a table in the library, we, about thirty of us, sit in council.

I learn something I'd heard but never experienced before: Arabs introduce themselves by telling you they are the mother or father of one of their children, perhaps their eldest, then they tell you how many children they have. They do this with a pride and joy I have never seen before. Only one woman has one child. Everyone else has at least five.

There is a feeling of festivity as the women, beautifully dressed and wearing elegant head scarves, laugh and joke among themselves. They are eager to talk. Only the woman with one child has trouble speaking. When I turn to her, I notice she is the only woman wearing black, and that her eyes are tearing. Unable to speak, she hands me instead a photograph she has been holding in her lap. She is a brown-skinned woman of African descent, as some Palestinians (to my surprise) are; the photograph is of her daughter, who looks European. The child looks about six years old. A student of ballet, she is dressed in a white tutu and is dancing. Her mother tries to speak but still cannot, as I sit holding her arm. It is another woman who explains: during the bombardment, the child was hit in the arm, the leg, and the chest and bled to death in her mother's arms. The mother and I embrace, and throughout our meeting I hold the photograph of the child, while the mother draws her chair closer to mine.

What do we talk about?
We talk about hatred.

But before we talk about hatred, I want to know about head scarves. What's the deal about wearing the scarf? Why do so many women wear it? I am aware of some of the religious reasons for wearing the *hijab*, and certainly no item of clothing has been more recently discussed, on several continents. I have learned of the prophet Mohammed's demand that his own wives be veiled, to protect them from the gaze of visitors and strangers, and of course the ongoing discussions regarding *hijab* wearing in England and France have been much in the news. There is also the brutal insistence in some Muslim countries that women cover themselves to demonstrate submission to religious, and male, authority. However, I am curious to know what grassroots Arab women think about the scarf, assuming as I do that most items of clothing have a use before religion claims one for them, as is proven by what the women share. I am told something I've never considered: in desert countries most of one's hydration is lost at the back of the neck, which can quickly lead to heatstroke, so a head scarf that wraps around the neck is essential to block this loss. The top of the head is covered because if a woman is living a traditional life and is outside a lot, the sun beats down on it. This causes headache, dizziness, nausea, stroke, and other health problems. In Gaza, one of the women points out, there are many women who do not wear scarves, primarily because they work in offices. This is true of the women in whose home we are sheltered. They seem to own a lot of scarves that they drape about themselves casually, just as my friends and I might do in the United States.

Because I have shaved my head a week or so before going to Gaza, I understand exactly the importance of the head scarf. Without a covering on my head I cannot bear the sun for more than a few minutes. And, indeed, one of the first gifts I receive from an anonymous Palestinian woman is a thick black and red embroidered scarf, which I wear everywhere, gratefully.

Our host tells us a story about the uglier side of the head-scarf business: On the first day of bombing she was working downstairs in the basement and wasn't aware that her apartment building was next to one that was being shelled. When the policemen came to clear her building, and she stepped out of the elevator, one of the police, a political and religious conservative, was taken aback at the sight of her bare head. So much so that, instead of instantly helping her to shelter, he called a colleague to come and witness her attire. Or lack thereof. He was angry with her for not wearing a head scarf, though Israeli rockets were tearing into buildings all around them. And what can we do but sigh along with her, as she relates this experience with appropriate shrugs and grimaces of exasperation. Backwardness is backwardness, wherever it occurs, and explains lack of progressive movement in some afflicted societies, whether under siege or not.

17. IT FEELS FAMILIAR

One of the triumphs of the civil rights movement is that when you travel through the South today you do not feel over-whelmed by a residue of grievance and hate. This is the legacy of people brought up in the Christian tradition, true believers of every word Jesus had to say on the issues of justice, loving kindness, and peace. This dovetailed nicely with what we learned of Gandhian nonviolence, brought into the movement by Bayard Rustin, a gay strategist for the civil rights movement. A lot of thought went into how to create "the beloved community" so that our country would not be stuck with violent hatred between black and white, and with the con-tinuous spectacle, and suffering, of communities going up in flames. The progress is astonishing and I will always love Southerners, black and white, for the way we have all grown. Ironically, though there was so much suffering and despair as the struggle for justice tested us, it is in this very "backward" part of our country today that one is most likely to find simple human helpfulness, thoughtfulness, and disinterested courtesy.

I speak a little about this American history, but it isn't history that these women know. They're too young. They've never been taught it. It feels irrelevant. Following their example of speaking of their families, I talk about my Southern parents' teachings during our experience of America's apartheid years, when white people owned and controlled all the resources and the land, in addition to the political, legal, and military apparatus, and used their power to intimidate black people in the most barbaric and merciless ways. These whites who tormented us daily were like Israelis who have cut down millions of trees planted by Arab Palestinians, stolen

Palestinian water, even topsoil. Forcing Palestinians to use separate roads from those they use themselves, they have bulldozed innumerable villages, houses, mosques, and in their place built settlements for strangers who have no connection whatsoever with Palestine: settlers who have been the most rabidly anti-Palestinian of all, attacking the children, the women, everyone, old and young alike, viciously.

What is happening here feels very familiar, I tell them. When something similar was happening to us in Mississippi, Georgia, Alabama, and Louisiana, I say, our parents taught us to think of the racists as we thought of any other disaster: to deal with that disaster as best we could, but not to attach to it by allowing ourselves to hate. This was a tall order, and as I'm talking I begin to understand, as if for the first time, why some of our parents' prayers were so long and fervent as they stayed there on their knees in church. And why people often wept, and fainted, and why there was so much tenderness as people deliberately silenced themselves, or camouflaged atrocities done to or witnessed by themselves, instead using representative figures from the Bible.

At the end of the table across from me is a woman who looks like Oprah's twin. In fact, earlier she had said to me: Alice, tell Oprah to come see us. We will take good care of her. I promise I will email Oprah and on returning home do so. She laughs, this handsome woman, then speaks earnestly. We don't hate Israelis, Alice, she says, quietly. What we hate is being bombed, watching our little ones live in fear, burying them, being starved to death, and being driven from our land. We hate this eternal crying out to the world to open its eyes and ears to the truth of what is happening, and being ignored. Israelis, no.

If they stopped humiliating and torturing us, if they stopped taking everything we have, including our lives, we would hardly think about them at all. Why would we?

18. OVERWHELM

There is a sense of overwhelm, trying to bring comfort to someone whose sleeping child has been killed and buried, a few weeks ago, up to her neck in rubble. Or to a mother who has lost fifteen members of her family, all her children, grandchildren, brothers and sisters, her husband. What does one say to people whose families came out of their shelled houses waving white flags of surrender only to be shot down anyway? To mothers whose children are, at this moment, playing in the white phosphorous-laden rubble that, after twenty-two days of bombing, is everywhere in Gaza? White phosphorus, once on the skin, never stops burning. There is really nothing to say. Nothing to say to those who, back home in America, don't want to hear the news.

Nothing to do, finally, but dance.

19. DANCE

The women and I and everyone with us from CODEPINK went across the hall to a big common room where music was turned up full volume. At first I sat exchanging smiles and murmurs with an ancient grandmother who was knitting booties, and who gave me two pairs for my own grandchildren. Sitting didn't last. Without preamble I was pulled to my feet by several women at once, and the dance was on. Sorrow, loss, pain, suffering, all pounded into the floor for over an hour. Sweat flowing, wails and tears around the room. And then, the rising that always comes from such dancing; the sense of joy, unity, solidarity, and gratitude to be in the best place one could be on earth, with sisters who have experienced the full measure of disaster and have the heart to rise above it. The feeling of love was immense. The ecstasy, sublime. I was conscious of exchanging and receiving Spirit in the dance. I also knew that this

Spirit, which I have encountered in Mississippi, Georgia, the Congo, Cuba, Rwanda, and Burma, among other places, this Spirit that knows how to dance in the face of disaster, will never be crushed. It is as timeless as the wind. We think it is only inside our bodies, but we also inhabit it. Even when we are unaware of its presence internally, it wears us like a cloak.

20. THEY BROKE MY HOUSE

I could have gone home then. I had learned what I came to know: that humans are an amazing lot. That to willfully harm any one of us is to damage us all. That hatred of ourselves is the root cause of any harm done to others, others so like us! And that we are lucky to live at a time when all lies will be exposed, along with the relief of not having to serve them any longer. But I did not go home. I went instead to visit the homeless.

Coming out of a small group of tents that

had absolutely nothing inside them—no bedding, no food, no water—were middle-aged and elderly people who looked as if their sky had fallen. It had. An old, old man, leaning on a stick, met me as I trudged up a hill so I might see the extent of the devastation. Vast. Look, look! He said to me in English, Come look at my house! He was wearing dusty cotton trousers and an old army great coat. I felt dragged along by the look in his eyes. He led me to what had been his house. From the remains, it had obviously been a large and spacious dwelling; now he and his wife lived between two of the fallen walls that made a haphazard, upside-down V. She looked as stunned and as lost as he did. There was not a single usable item visible.

Near what must have been the front entrance, the old man placed me directly in front of the remains of bulldozed trees. They broke my house, he said, by bombing it, and then they came with bulldozers and they broke my lemon and olive trees. The

Israeli military has destroyed over two and a half million olive and fruit trees alone since 1948. Having planted many trees myself, I shared his sorrow about the fate of these ones. I imagined them alive and sparkling with life, offering olives and lemons, the old man and his wife able to sit in the shade of the trees in the afternoons, with a cup of tea there in the evenings.

You speak English, I observed. Yes, he said, I was once in the British Army. I supposed this was during the time Britain controlled Palestine, before 1948. We walked along in silence, as I did what I had come to do: witness. CODEPINK members and my companion and I walked through the rubble of demolished homes, schools, medical centers, and factories. After the bombing the Israelis had indeed bulldozed everything so that I was able to find just one piece of evidence that beauty had flourished on this hillside, a shard from a piece of colorful tile, about the size of my hand. Someone in our group wanted it, and I gave it to her. They had taken pains to pulverize what they had destroyed.

Coming upon another group of tents, I encountered an old woman sitting on the ground in what would have been, perhaps, the doorway of her demolished, pulverized home. She was clean and impeccably dressed, the kind of old woman who is known and loved and respected by everyone in the community, as my own mother had been. Her eyes were dark and full of life. She talked to us freely.

I gave her a gift I had brought, and she thanked me. Looking into my eyes she said: May God protect you from the Jews. When the young Palestinian interpreter told me what she'd said, I responded: It's too late, I already married one. I said this partly because, like so many Jews in America, my former husband could not tolerate criticism of Israel's behavior toward the Palestinians. Our very different positions on what is happening now in Palestine/Israel, and what has been happening for over fifty years, has been perhaps our most severe disagreement. It is a subject we have never been able to rationally discuss. He does not see the racist treatment of Palestinians as the same racist treatment of blacks and some Jews that he fought against so nobly in Mississippi, and that he objected to in his own Brooklyn-based family. When his younger brother found out he was seeing me, a black person, the brother bought and nailed over an entire side of his bedroom the largest Confederate flag my former husband and I had ever seen. His brother, a young Jewish man who had never traveled South, and had perhaps learned most of what he knew about black history from *Gone with the Wind*, expressed his contempt for black people in this way. His mother, when told of our marriage, sat shiva, which declared my husband dead.

These were people who knew how to hate, and how to severely punish others, even those beloved, as he was. This is one reason I understand the courage it takes for some

Jews to speak out against Israeli brutality and against what they know are crimes against humanity. Most Jews who know their own history see how relentlessly the Israeli government is attempting to turn Palestinians into the "new Jews," patterned on Jews of the Holocaust era, as if someone must hold that place in order for Jews to avoid it.

21. JEWISH FRIENDS OF THE PLANET

Lucky for me, my husband's family are not the only Jews I know, having met Howard Zinn, my history teacher at Spelman College in 1961, as my very first (secular) Jew, and later poet Muriel Rukeyser at Sarah Lawrence College, who, like Grace Paley, the short-story writer, raises her voice against the Israeli occupation of Palestine and the horrible mistreatment of the Palestinian people. There are my Jewish friends of the planet: Amy Goodman, Jack Kornfield, Noam Chomsky, Medea Benjamin, and Barbara Lubin, who are as piercing in their assessments of Israeli behavior as they have been of African or African-American or Indian or Chinese or Burmese behavior. I place my faith in them, and in others like us, who see how greed and brutality are not limited to any segment of humanity but will grow wherever it is unchecked, in any society. The people of Israel have not been helped by America's blind loyalty to their survival as a Jewish state by any means necessary. The very settlers, for whom they've used American taxpayer money to install on Palestinian land, turn out to be a scary lot, fighting not only against Palestinians, but also against Israelis, when they do not get their way. Israelis stand now exposed, the warmongers and peacemakers alike, as people who are ruled by leaders that the world considers irrational, vengeful, scornful of international law, and utterly frightening. There are differing opinions about this, of course, but my belief is that when a country primarily instills fear in the minds and hearts of the people of the world, it is no longer useful in joining the dialogue we need for saving the planet. There is no hiding what Israel has done or what it does on a daily basis to protect and extend its power. It uses weapons that cut off limbs without bleeding; into people's homes it drops bombs that never stop detonating in the bodies of anyone who is hit; it causes pollution so severe it is probable that Gaza may be uninhabitable for years to come, though Palestinians, having nowhere else to go, will have to live there.

This is a chilling use of power, supported by the United States of America, no small foe, if one stands up to it. No wonder most people prefer to look the other way during this genocide, hoping their disagreement with Israeli policies will not be noted.

Good Germans, good Americans, good Jews.

But, as our sister Audre Lorde liked to warn us: Our silence will not protect us. In the ongoing global climate devastation that is worsened by war activities, we will all suffer, and we will also be afraid.

22. THE WORLD KNOWS

The world knows it is too late for a two-state solution. This old idea, bandied about since at least the eighties, denounced by Israel for decades, isn't likely to become reality with the massive buildup of settlements all over what remains of Palestinian land. Ariel Sharon is having the last word: Jewish settlements exactly like a pastrami sandwich, with Palestinian life erased, as if it never existed, or crushed under the weight of a superior Israeli military presence, and a teaching of Jewish supremacy sure to stunt Palestinian identity among Arabs living in Israel.

What is to be done?
What is to be done? Our revered Tolstoy asked this question, speaking also of war

and peace. I believe there must be a one-state solution. Palestinians and Jews, who have lived together in peace in the past, must work together to make this a reality once again. This land (so soaked in Jewish and Palestinian blood, and with America's taxpayer dollars wasted on violence the majority of us would never, if we knew, support) must become, like South Africa, the secure and peaceful home of everyone who lives there. This will require that Palestinians, like Jews, have the right of return to their homes and their lands. Which will mean what Israelis most fear: Jews will be outnumbered and, instead of a Jewish state, there will be a Jewish, Muslim, Christian country, which is how Palestine functioned before the Europeans arrived. What is so awful about that?

The tribunals, the generals will no doubt say. But both South Africa and Rwanda present a model of restorative justice in their Truth and Reconciliation Commissions. Some crimes against humanity are so heinous nothing will ever rectify them. All we can do is attempt to understand their causes and do everything in our power to prevent them from happening, to anyone, ever again. Human beings are intelligent and, very often, compassionate. We can learn to heal ourselves without inflicting fresh wounds.

23. LIBERATION FOR THE TYRANT

Watching a video recently about Cuba's role in the ending of apartheid in South Africa, I was moved by the testimony of Pik Botha, once a high-ranking official of white South Africa. He talked about how liberating it had been when South Africa was forced to attend talks prior to negotiating Nelson Mandela's release from prison and the change from a fascist white supremacist regime to a democratic society. He said the feeling of not being hated and feared and treated like a leper everywhere he went was wonderful.

The talks were held in Egypt, and for the first time he felt welcomed by the Egyptians and took the opportunity to visit the pyramids and the Sphinx and to ride on a camel! As a white supremacist representative of a repressive, much hated government, he'd never felt relaxed enough to do that.

His words demonstrate what we all know in our hearts to be true: allowing freedom to others brings freedom to ourselves. It is true that what one reads in the papers sometimes about the birthing pains of the new South Africa can bring sadness, alarm, and near despair. But I doubt that anyone in South Africa wishes to return to the old days of injustice and violence that scarred whites and blacks and coloreds so badly.

Not just citizens of South Africa were demoralized, oppressed, and discouraged by white South Africa's behavior, but citizens of the world. Israel helped keep the racist regime in power in South Africa, giving it arms and expertise, and still the people of the world, in our outrage at the damage done to defenseless people, rose to the challenge of setting them free.

This is what is happening today in Palestine.

24. THE WORLD IS FINDING ITS VOICE

The world is, at last, finding its voice about everything that harms it. In this sense the twin teachers of catastrophic climate change (some of it caused by war) and the Internet have arrived to awaken the voice of even the most silenced. Though the horror of what we are witnessing in places like Rwanda and Congo and Burma and Palestine/Israel threatens our very ability to speak, we will speak. And, because almost everyone on the planet now acknowledges our collective slide into global disaster unless we profoundly change our ways, we will be heard.

"To the Editors of *Ms.* Magazine," in my book *In Search of Our Mothers' Gardens: Womanist Prose*, 1983. This is an essay/memo written a few weeks prior to the Israeli invasion of Lebanon and a few months before the Beirut massacres, in response to an article by Letty Cottin Pogrebin, "Anti-Semitism in the Women's Movement," which appeared in the June 1982 issue. I am writing about my refusal, as a woman of color, to be silenced and how black history supports this stance.

My interview in Gaza with reporters from *Democracy Now!* on YouTube.

"Sister Loss," an essay about the bombing of Gaza that appears on my blog: www.alicewalkersblog.com

Palestine: Peace Not Apartheid by President Jimmy Carter.

One Country: A Bold Proposal to End the Israeli-Palestinian Impasse by Ali Abunimah (probably the most important book to read on Palestinian/Israeli issues at this time). Abunimah gives a remarkably balanced account of Palestinian/Israeli history, as well as a convincing argument for choosing a one-state solution.

Palestine Inside Out: An Everyday Occupation by Saree Makdisi is a must read, but on a day when the reader is feeling strong. For this reader it brought almost too close memories of growing up in the American South, in the fifties and early sixties, when any white person could demand that you get off the sidewalk.

A People's History of the United States by Howard Zinn. Israel learned a lot of its behavior from America; this vital resource illustrates this.

A wide selection of Noam Chomsky's teachings on Israel and Palestine on YouTube.

The writings and taped lectures of Edward Said.

Interviews with Israeli soldiers on YouTube, Alternate Focus, AlterNet, World Focus, the BBC, and *Democracy Now!*

Movies: *The Battle of Algiers*, 1966, and *Waltz With Bashir*, 2009.

Alice Walker has published seven books of poetry: *Once*; *Revolutionary Petunias*; *Good Night, Willie Lee, I'll See You in the Morning*; *Horses Make a Landscape Look More Beautiful*; *Her Blue Body Everything We Know: Earthling Poems 1965–1990 Complete* (with previously unpublished poems); *Absolute Trust in the Goodness of the Earth*; and *A Poem Traveled Down My Arm: Poetry and Drawings*. Her eighth collection, *Hard Times Require Furious Dancing: A Year of Poems*, will be published in 2010. She has received numerous awards for her poetry and essays. Her novel *The Color Purple* won the Pulitzer Prize for Fiction in 1983.

Overcoming Speechlessness, discussing the trauma of disaster, sorrow, and loss always returns her to the writing of poetry, her first love and most enduring joy.

www.alicewalkersgarden.com

ABOUT SEVEN STORIES PRESS

Seven Stories Press is an independent book publisher based in New York City, with distribution throughout the United States, Canada, England, and Australia. We publish works of the imagination by such writers as Nelson Algren, Russell Banks, Octavia E. Butler, Ani DiFranco, Assia Djebar, Ariel Dorfman, Coco Fusco, Barry Gifford, Lee Stringer, and Kurt Vonnegut, to name a few, together with political titles by voices of conscience, including the Boston Women's Health Collective, Noam Chomsky, Angela Y. Davis, Human Rights Watch, Derrick Jensen, Ralph Nader, Gary Null, Project Censored, Barbara Seaman, Alice Walker, Gary Webb, and Howard Zinn, among many others. Seven Stories Press believes publishers have a special responsibility to defend free speech and human rights, and to celebrate the gifts of the human imagination, wherever we can. For additional information, visit www.sevenstories.com.